Stop The B.S. and Get it Done

WORKBOOK

Create, Sell and Promote
ANYTHING
in
7 STEPS

Tracy Balan

DEDICATION

To my better half —
Thank you for always
believing in me.

CONTENTS

"Once you replace negative thoughts with positive ones, you'll start having Positive Results!"

INTRODUCTION

It's time to stop the B.S.! But don't feel bad, I've been there. The number one challenge most people have is execution. I see it all the time. You have a great idea but don't know where to start!

Maybe you're a great note taker, reader and even ask great questions. But you can't decide where to begin; you aren't sure how to put the pieces together, or you can't stay motivated and focused long enough to finish.

Well, this book is the ANSWER! This book is about action and will serve you as a fill-in the blanks workbook and guide to create, sell and promote successfully. You will find that *Stop the B.S. and Get It Done* will provide you with not only the discipline to create but will also help you on the road of self-discovery. And by the end of this workbook, you will have a total understanding of how to make "**BANK**" off your passion, purpose and talents.

You can modify this workbook according to your needs and use it over and over again. You can complete this workbook in 7 days, by doing a Step a day or you can take your time and complete this in 7 weeks or 7 months. The one thing is you must **GET IT DONE**! With some consistency, prioritization, creativity and focus you can expect in 7 steps to have a complete and sellable product/service to take to market.

Quick Note: Thought-out this workbook you will sometimes see the word **BANK** in bold, this means money! Some people like to say "coins" when they are referring to money, but I like Bank, because who wants coins when you can own the **BANK**!

ARE YOU READY?

Before you get started on the first step, I want to ask you the all-important question:

Are you sure you are ready to do this?

I will assume if you're still reading, that your answer is: "Hell Yes!" But I will not sugarcoat this; this will require some hard work and dedication, that I know you are more than capable of doing I just need you to believe it too.

Above all, remember to give yourself some grace as you go through the steps, the last thing you need is more pressure. So, breathe deeply and get ready to enjoy the creation process.

Keep this quote in mind as you go through the steps:

"Strength does not come from what you can do. It comes from doing the things you thought you could not do."

-unknown

Keep me updated with your new Products or Services by tagging me **@TracyBalan** *or* **#StopTheBS** – *Can't wait to see what you create!* - TB

"The desire to create is one of the deepest yearnings of the human soul."

-Elder Uchtdorf

Step 1

Let's start with the most important thing:

How to Create?
and
What to Create?

To understand how to do this, you must first learn more about yourself.

On the following pages, you will be answering questions to help you define your wants, needs, passion, and purpose; This will help you understand what makes you great and how to make "**BANK**" doing it.

21 Questions

1. What is your Passion and What is your purpose?

   a. Do you know the difference?

2. What else do you think you would need to learn to take your passions or purpose to the next level?

3. What motivates you?

    a. What about this keeps you motivated?

4. What makes you happiest in your life?

    a. What excites you?

5. What are you ridiculously good at? (The thing that you do great with little to no effort)

6. What amount of money do you think you would need to make, to pursue your Passion or Purpose?

7. What do you have an interest in or find yourself researching often?

      a. What do you explore the most on the internet?

8. Who inspires you? Why?

      a. Who are your mentors?

9. What do you feel most comfortable talking about?

10. What have you taught yourself? List everything you can think of:

11. What's the first magazine you'd pick up at the grocery store?

12. What do people always ask you to help with?

13. Your co-workers and friends always say you are great at _____, because _____.

14. What do you find the most joy helping people with?

15. What 3 dream businesses can you imagine having, that would firmly embody you and your core beliefs? (No limits)

16. If you had a free Saturday that had to be spent "working" on something, you would choose _____, because _____.

17. What would a dream day look like for you from start to finish?

18. What commitments or roadblocks are holding you back from working on what you love?

19. When was the last time you massively over-delivered on something?

      a. What was it and why did you work so damn hard?

20. When was the last time you couldn't sleep because you were so excited about what you had to work on?

a. What was it?

21. When you retire, you want to be known for
_____,
because_____.

There Is No Elevator To Success.
You Have To Take The Stairs!

Aha!

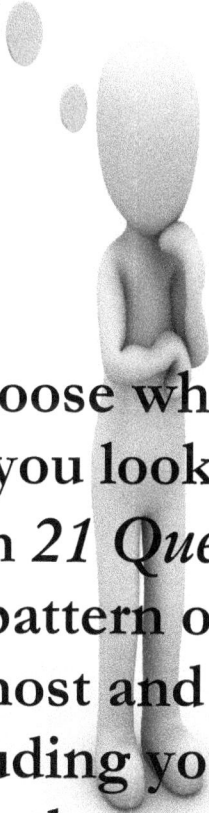

It's time to Choose what you will create. If you look at all your answers in *21 Questions*, you will see a pattern of what interest you most and what everyone including yourself already knows makes you great!

Top 3 Things To Create

Write your choices above the doors

Take a look at your top three choices. Which of these sparks a fire in you? Which one will drive you for the next 6 Steps? What makes it a great fit for you now? What will it mean to you when you finish?

(write your answers below)

Moment of Truth

For The Next 6 Steps You Will Create:

People Will Pay You for This Product or Service Because:

1.

2.

3.

4.

5.

6.

7.

Step 2 at a Glance

Now that you have chosen what you will create; let's look at what you will be working on next.

You don't need to answer all these questions now, but you do need to start thinking about the answers to them.

1. Who is your market?

2. What are their needs?

3. Who are your competitors?

4. What will make your product/service different or better?

5. What will people love about your product/service?

6. What will you need to do to bring your product/service to market?

7. What will your mission statement be?

<u>Notes</u>

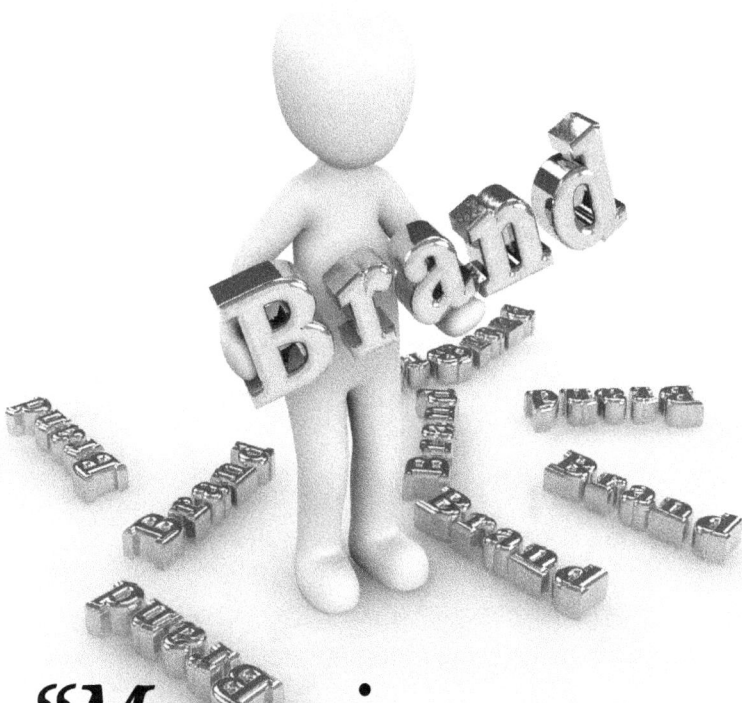

"Managing your brand is not a singular event but is a continuous process."

-Unknown

Developing

Step 2

If you don't know where you're going, how do you know when you get there?

The same question can be asked about any task, goal or vision. In Step 2 you will need to keep this in mind as you do the work to find out and create a solid plan on your: Market, Competitors, the Mission Statement and the Company Blueprint.

Define Your Market

Taking the time to define your potential clients down to their very core will put you leaps and bounds ahead of your competitors. Understanding how to market to potential clients will not only help you in the future; but will be a key tool in figuring out areas of improvement for the products/services you create.

Demographic
Age:
Location:
Sex:
Ethnicity:
Income Level:
Education Level:
Occupation:
Marital/Family Status:
Kids:
Religion:
Political:

Geographic
Where do they live (now, previously)? Country, region?

Do they live in an urban or rural environment?

What language is spoken?

What is the climate? The seasons?

Psychographic
Are they satisfied with their job? Y/N

What type of lifestyle?

Their social class (lower, middle, upper class)?

What is their current health level?

What are their:
    a) Goals:

    b) Beliefs:

    c) Interests:

    d) Habits:

    e) Values:

    f) Attitudes:

    g) Hobbies

How would you sum up their feelings about money?

What is their biggest expense each month? 2nd biggest?

Behavioral

What occasions are important to your potential Clients?

Are they loyal (already fans of your genre/topic)?

Where are they in terms of readiness to buy? (Already buying similar products/services or needs some persuasion?)

Who or What else will influence their buying decisions for a product/service like yours?

What are their buying patterns? (Buy on impulse, or look for value?)

Where and how do they read? (Mobile? eBooks? Print?)

Which magazines or Blogs do they read?

What would make them trust a new product, service, blog, or brand?

What would make them share your product/service information with others?

What are their primary needs and concerns in life?

Where do they shop online or in store?

What type of computer do they use?

How are they most likely to first hear about products/services like yours?

What type of device will they most likely access your brand from first?

What will make them trust and respect someone in your field?

What social media networks do they use? How often?

Instagram: LinkedIn:

Twitter: Snapchat:

YouTube: Periscope:

Google+:   Facebook:

Pinterest: Other:

Other: Other:

On which network(s) are they most likely to share information or recommendations with friends?

List the top three reasons they might follow you online or look for your content regularly:
1.

2.

3.

Needs & Wants

How does your product/service help or serve your market?

How will your product/service help your markets top three frustrations or desires right now?

1.

2.

3.

Who or what is currently trying or filling the needs of your market?

What will people love about your product/service?

List three questions people are most likely to have about your products/services?

1.

2.

3.

<u>Notes</u>

(add any additional notes about your market here)

The Competition

Now it's time to power up social media and the web. Do a little reach on your competition by using Facebook, Twitter, Instagram, Amazon, Google and more.

If you are selling something digital like apps, online courses, eBooks, podcasts, look online for similar products/services like yours. Look through the individual sites and review their course syllabus and information.

If you are selling something tangible like clothes, hair, toys, etc., visit both the online website and store (if possible). Also, purchase something small to see how long it takes to get to you and check out their return procedures.

If you are selling a service like consulting, virtual assistant, web design, look to see what your competitors are offering and for how long. Make sure to take a good look at how they choose to package the services offered.

For all products and services:

When you visit the individual sites make sure you write down everything that stands out to you. Compare prices but know when you should charge more and when to charge less. Look at your competitor's reviews. First, check the negative reviews then check the good reviews and see how you can improve upon them. Don't just think about making your product/service better, make it stand out!

"You Can't Look At The Competition
And Say You're Going
To Do It Better.
You Have To Look At The Competition
And Say You're Going
To Do It Differently."

- Steve Jobs

Who are your top 3 competitors? (only competitors on the same level as you right now. As your products/services grow you will need to update this list.)

1.

2.

3.

What products/services do they have that are similar to yours?

What are their products/services missing?

What would you do differently or better?

What are their prices?

What are their return policies?

What makes your product/service different or better?

What will people love about your product/service?

Think of 7 creative ways you can make the competition an ally by doing promotions, affiliate programs & more:
(This step may sound a little crazy, but have you ever heard of the saying: "Keep your enemies close"? Well, that's what you are doing. The most successful people understand that there is enough business to go around and your competitors can sometimes be your best resources.)

1.

2.

3.

4.

5.

6.

7.

Notes

(add any additional notes about your competitors here)

The Mission Statement

Definition: *A short written statement of your business goals and philosophies (no more than 3 – 4 sentences).*

Now that you know the definition of a mission statement let talk about the *"Why"* of making one.

Even if you are a small business owner, freelancer, or moonlighting your business for extra cash – to make **"BANK"**, you will benefit from taking some time to craft this statement. Let me break it down!

Traditionally, a mission statement is a tool used as part of the business planning process to outline the purpose of its existence. In my opinion, the mission statement helps you hold yourself accountable. It helps you realize when you are off-track and need to turn around. It also helps you make decisions about the company that will keep you on track with what your goals and objectives are.

Your mission statement doesn't have to be clever or catchy--just accurate. It doesn't have to be long or detailed, just precise and to the point. Now if it happens to be clever and catchy then you have yourself a Win – Win!

Here is my formula for a great mission statement: **The 4W's**

Who x What x Why x What

Using all your answers from the sections *Define Your Market* and *The Competition*, come up with no more than one sentence for each question below. You will then take your four sentences to make an accurate and precise mission statement.

Who - Who are you and who are you creating this for?

What - What are you creating and What problem does it fix?

Why - Why do you do it?

What - What do you stand for?

Examples of Great Mission Statements:

Google – "To organize the world's information and make it universally accessible and useful."

Amazon – "We seek to be Earth's most customer-centric company for four primary customer sets: consumers, sellers, enterprises, and content creators."

TED - "Spread Ideas."

Walmart – "Helps people around the world save money and live better -- anytime and anywhere -- in retail stores, online and through their mobile devices."

Universal Health Services, Inc. – "To provide superior quality healthcare services that: Patients recommend to family and friends, Physicians prefer for their patients, Purchasers select for their clients, Employees are proud of, and Investors seek for long-term returns."

Your Mission Statement:

*Quick Break: Jump on social media and share your mission statement with the world. Don't forget to tag me too **@TracyBalan** or **#StopTheBS** – Can't wait to see what you came up with. -**TB***

<u>Notes</u>

Blueprint

The blueprint will be your plan, design, diagram, drawing, sketch, map, or layout. All a representation of the ideas and steps needed to be done to create or setup to bring your product/service to market.

You will need a pack of index cards. Separate it into three stacks; you will only need two stacks out of the three to start. Now take one stack of index cards and cut them in half. You will now have one stack of whole size index cards and two stacks of half size index cards.

Whole   **Half**

You will be using theses index cards to map out the major topics and subtopics of your products/services. Keep in mind when creating your blueprints all the things that you want to improve on in the market that you are focused on.

Let's get started:

Step 1 –Get a timer out and set it for 7 minutes. Using the whole cards, write down all the main topics or points on individual cards. Write down everything you can think of, holding nothing back for those 7 minutes.

Step 2 –Review your mission statement then go through the cards you have written. Consolidate topics that are similar and eliminate anything that does not fit.

Step 3 –Take the note cards you have narrowed down and spread it in front of you. Arrange them in the order that you will be laying out or rolling out your product/Service.

Step 4 – Get your timer out again but, this time, set it for 5 minutes. On the individual half, cards write down all the points you want to convey on the main topics. Think of your half cards as subcategories. Reset your timer for each whole index card topic.

Step 5 – Repeat **Step 2** for all half cards.

Step 6 –Review and rearrange all your index cards both whole and half cards until you have an order that best suits the product/service you are selling.

Step 7 –Input your new Blueprint into a spreadsheet. You can use the one I have supplied for you on *page.36,* or you can create one for yourself.

Main Topics

Subtopics

Example

Note: These steps will have different meanings depending on what you are creating. You can use this system in many different ways. Examples are website layouts, book chapters, courses, clothing design, app designs and promotional strategies just to name a few.

Blueprint Spreadsheet

The Blueprint spreadsheet will help you understand how much work is needed; this is also a great way to keep up with outsourced work and their due dates.

Topics –Write your main topics and subtopics.

Process -What will need to be done for each topic or subtopic.

Notes -Extra things like outsourced names, vendors, etc.

Due -Dues dates on when things are due, so you don't miss a beat!

Topics	Process	Notes	Due
Main topic	What needs to be done for this to be complete.	Is this outsourced, are their more steps needed.	01/01/16
Subtopic			
Subtopic			
Subtopic			
Main Topic			
Subtopic			
Subtopic			Example

idea ⇢ plan ⇢ action

"Failing to plan
is
planning to fail!"
-Alan Lakein

	Process	Notes	Due

Step 3 at a Glance

In step three you will be playing the name game. Figuring out your name and its meaning in the market you choose to sell in will be one of the keys to your success.

Answer or just keep in mind the questions asked below.

1. What will you name your product/service?

2. What meaning does the name have?

3. What feeling do you want to leave with your audience after they purchase your product/service?

4. What words or sentences best describe the feeling you want left with your consumers?

<u>Notes</u>

"You never learn anything, Talking. You only learn things from asking Questions."

-Tracy Balan

The Name Game

Step 3

It's time for the name game! Picking the right name for your product/service is one of the most important decisions you are going to make. Regardless of how amazing what you create is, people will only remember two things: the name and how they feel about the product/service.

With an understanding of your brand promise, and what influences your clients, you will be ready to pick a name. Even if you aren't a creative person the following outline can help you come up with a name people can remember and a brand promise people will trust.

Quick Note: When you're separating the good names from the bad, consider naming expert, Alexandra Watkins', Scratch principle: you should consider your name less than ideal if it's: Spelling-challenged, A Copycat, Restrictive, Annoying, Too Tame, Cursed by Jargon, or Hard to Pronounce.

When you're picking a name for a business, product or a service, you have a number of options:

1. Use the founder or inventor's name (*ex: Hewlett-Packard*)
2. Describe what you do (*ex: Southwest Airlines*)
3. Describe an experience or image (*ex: Sprint*)
4. Take a word out of context (*ex: Apple*)
5. Make up a word (*ex: Google*)

You will also need to keep in mind this formula:

Functionality x Memorability x Simplicity

Functionality -Describes the nature of your business by its name.

ex: *YouTube, Cable News Network [CNN], Burger King*

Memorability -A deliberate and creative combination of words. The quality or state of being easy to remember or worth remembering.

ex: *Kodak, Pinterest, Wikipedia*

Simplicity -Something which is easy to understand or explain

ex: *Amazon, Nike, Fedex*

To help with the process of picking a name go through the list of sites below. They will also help you narrow down website availabilities too.

(Answer the questions on the following page to help you configure keywords to use on these websites.)

1. Bust-A-Name
http://www.bustaname.com/?rid=8726750

This is a great tool for brainstorming not only brand names but domain names as well. Enter in your initial keyword ideas to help generate great name ideas.

2. Shopify Business Name Generator
http://1.shopifytrack.com/aff_c?offer_id=2&aff_id=3394

A free tool from Shopify that automatically combines your keyword with other words to generate a major list of available domain names. Also, a great way to pick out product /service names.

3. Lean Domain Search
http://www.leandomainsearch.com/

This is a good website that matches your keyword with other words to generate a list of available domain names. You can choose to sort the results by popularity, length or alphabetically, as well as select whether you want the results to start or end with your keyword.

4. Wordoid
http://wordoid.com/
This site is a naming tool that supplies you with a random list of made-up words. If you're looking for a creative name that's brand-able but doesn't necessarily need to make sense, then you might find this tool helpful.

5. GoSpaces Business Name Generator
https://gospaces.com/tools/business-name-generator
This website helps you find a name for just about anything. Just simply put in a keyword related to your business, and get started.

What are three things you want people to feel when they talk about your product/service?

1.

2.

3.

Write down three phrases for your product/service:
(Phrase - a small group of words standing together as a conceptual unit, typically forming a component of a clause. Ex: "his favorite phrase is "it's a pleasure."")

1.

2.

3.

What are three unique things about your product/Service:

1.

2.

3.

Using what you learned on *page.41* and the answers on *page.42*, write down your top 5 options:

1.

2.

3.

4.

5.

What are your top 5 website options? *(Skip this step if not applicable)*
1.

2.

3.

4.

5.

"The purpose of a
BUSINESS
is to create a
CUSTOMER
who creates
CUSTOMERS"

- unknown

<u>Notes</u>

Elimination

Let's start the process of elimination. Use the questions that follow to narrow down your top picks till you are only left with one name. *(use search engines to do quick searches and your notes from **pages.41 - 44**)*

1. Does the name consider gender? *(Are you selling a product/service that is for women, men or both? If gender specific which one matches?)*

2. Are there competitors in your category with similar names?

3. Are there products not similar to you with the same name? *(if so, did you intentionally want that?)*

4. Is it easy to pronounce, understand, and remember?

5. Are there any negative connotations or associations with the names you have chosen? *(This is something to note because if you are looking to trademark or copyright your name now or later, it can cause big problems)*

6. Are the names chosen trademarked or copyrighted? **(Check trademarks:** http://tmsearch.uspto.gov **Check Copyrights:** http://www.copyright.gov/records/ **)**

7. Is your product/service name, or a deceptively similar name, already filed with your County Clerk's Office or State Commerce Division as a business? *(you can do a web search for this too or look up the local number to call)*

8. Is your name available on all the social media sites you want to use to promote your Brand? *(You only need to check this if you want your brand to have its own social media profiles.)*

Your Final Product/Service Name:

Quick Break: Jump on social media and share your product/service name with the world. Don't forget to tag me too @TracyBalan or #StopTheBS – Can't wait to see what you came up with. -TB

Brand Promise

Definition: *A brand promise is one that connects your purpose, your positioning, your strategy, your product / service and your client's experience. It enables you to deliver your brand in a way that connects emotionally with your clients.*

In this workbook, you will be using your brand promise as your introduction to your product/service. This is where you get your consumer excited about what they are going to experience with your product or service. This is where you set the tone to keep them going. This will happen with one or all three elements depending on your brand. These elements are *Audio, Visual, or Written*.

To help create a great brand promise answer the questions below and keep in mind key elements on how you will display this in the intro of your product or service. You also need to keep in mind the acronym **L.C.E.: Lifestyle – Creative – Emotion**.

1. The first thing you need to do is emphasize the things that will make your consumer buy. Write a maximum of three sentences that reflexes, what will cause your sales. *(***Ex - Product:** You were looking for a solution to your foot ache problems when wearing high heels. You no longer wanted to forgo style for comfort. So you turn to Insert Comfort for…)

Now let's work with the acronym **L.C.E.**:
(Write one sentence for each acronym)

2. **Lifestyle** – In today's time, it's important that you invoke the lifestyle in your brand if you want to compete with your competitors. Your brand promise has to show that it is contributing to your potential consumer's way of life. (**Ex - Product:** Finally, a workbook that can help you get it done with solid steps at your pace and in any environment: sitting in a waiting room, bus ride home, breakroom at the office, just to name a few.)

3. **Creative** – Be creative in a way that makes your consumer feel like something new is being presented to them (this is especially important if you have a similar product/service to someone else). (**Ex - Service:** This life coaching sessions with help you both mentally and physically. As a bonus after finishing 3 one on ones with your life coach you will receive two follow-up sessions three months after your last.)

4. **Emotions** – This is where you close the deal and show the consumer why they are so connected to your product.

Some of the best consumers are the ones that have an emotional attachment to your product/service. (**Ex - Service:** The feeling of knowing you finally have found someone who not only understands you but does not judge you. Think about this as you work with your therapist..)

Now use all your sentences to compose a solid Brand Promise

Your Brand Promise:

Congrats by answering these questions you now have your brand promise and your introduction page for your product/service. You will be using this as a reference to look back to as you continue to work through the steps of what you will be creating. You should also take note that this will also be a great way to make sure you stay on track.

*Quick Break: Jump on social media and share your product/service answers with the world. Don't forget to tag me too **@TracyBalan** or **#StopTheBS** – Can't wait to see what you came up with. -**TB***

Step 4 at a Glance

It is time to start the creation process. You will be using the research and answers from steps 2 and 3 to build a creative guide to get you smoothly and consistently through step 5, 6 and 7.

Answer or just keep in mind the questions asked below.

1. What will be your product /service theme colors?

2. What font styles do you like?

3. What images will represent your product /services?

4. How will you set the tone for your product/service?

5. What tools will you need to execute the creation of your product/service?

<u>Notes</u>

"The best way to predict the future is to create it."

-Peter Drucker

Creative Guide

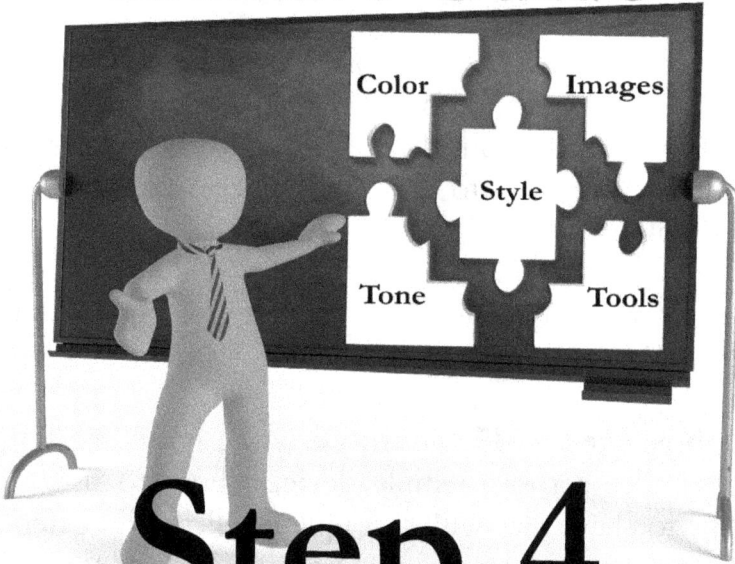

Color   Images

Style

Tone   Tools

Step 4

Okay, you have done quite a bit of work. And you are probably like: "Dame girl what next? You want a kidney?" – Short answer: Yes, lol! But seriously now it's time to form your creative guide. I will lay out the formula, and you will put the pieces together and learn all the tools you need for your product/service.

A lot of time people will start a project and right in the middle figure out they are missing a lot of different pieces. This step will help you to miss nothing. We are going to pick logos, colors, images, the web hosting company and more.

So let's get creative!

Collect and Organize

The first step is to choose a place to store and organize all your great ideas and content that inspires you. There are tons of digital tools out there, but the list below is some of my favs. Feel free to use whichever makes you most comfortable.

Your Computer (free): You can use your computer and create different folders to store all ideas and inspiration.

Dropbox (free - $15 monthly): is the go-to solution for syncing files across multiple devices. Easy to use, allows groups to share files with a couple of clicks and offers few settings for you to mess up. Dropbox is great for storing, photos, documents and videos.
https://db.tt/ILwuzoT1

Basecamp 3 (free - $79 monthly): is more like a project manager and is great when you have a team. Depending on your account level you can give employees and clients a login to upload and edit different files. Great for people who have teams in other states but want one platform to communicate, without a ton of back and forth emails.
https://basecamp.com/

Dropmark (Free - $5 monthly): organize links, files, and text notes into collections and decide who sees what. Keep your content private, invite friends, or go public. Each collection has a short, shareable link. Great to use when for filing lots of links and images.
http://www.dropmark.com/

Trello (free - $21 monthly): keeps track of everything, from the big picture to the minute details. More of a great online tool for organizing. I would recommend using after we have narrowed down your ideas and inspirations. https://trello.com/

Once you have chosen how you will store your ideas and inspirations, I want you to create three folders labeled by these categories: **Theme, Images, and References**.

Theme

In this category, you will be looking up fonts, colors and layouts. Your product/service should have a consistent theme not only on your website but, on social media too.

Quick Note: Choosing colors for your brand shouldn't be about your favorite color, but rather what you want your logo to say about your company. A startup could offer the most innovative software, the most disruptive service, the greatest thing ever available for purchase in the history of life — but if the company color scheme is off-putting, its clients might decide to shop elsewhere.

Some tools to help you find inspirations:

Colors:
    a) https://www.google.com/ -Using the search words: Colors meaning for your business
    b) https://color.adobe.com -Write down the hex code (6-digit color code – ex: #008008) or RGB information of each color you like.
    c) https://www.pinterest.com/ -Using the search words: Color Schemes

Fonts: (Just make sure your font will be compatible on all platforms)

a) https://www.google.com/fonts
b) http://www.dafont.com/
c) https://www.pinterest.com/ -Using the search words: Fonts

Layouts:

a) https://creativemarket.com – Is a great site for themes, graphics, fonts and more.
b) http://market.envato.com/ - Is great for all creative projects
c) https://www.google.com/ -Using the search words: layout design inspiration
d) https://www.canva.com/ -Is great for creating your layouts and other creative projects. This site is easy to use and great when you want to keep overhead down of hiring a graphic designer.

Images

In this category, you will be looking for images that not only inspire you but are a good fit for your product/ service. Also, a great place to store logo ideas and future social media post images.

a) https://pixabay.com/ - all images and videos on Pixabay are released free of copyrights under Creative Commons CC0
b) https://www.google.com/images
c) Magazines, Books, other Websites and more.

References

In this category, you should add magazine articles, book references, quotes, and links to references that will help you complete the setup and creation of your product/service.

"Data by itself is useless. Data is only useful if you apply it."

-Todd Park

After you have organized everything into categories, it is time to narrow things down. Go through your folders and eliminate things that don't seem to fit the main theme of your product/service.

What is your color scheme?
(2-4 colors to be used consistently thought-out your product/service text, titles, & Social Post)

1._____   2._____

hex code:_____   hex code:_____

3._____   4._____

hex code:_____   hex code:_____

*Quick Break: Jump on social media and share your color scheme with the world. Don't forget to tag me too **@TracyBalan** or **#StopTheBS** – Can't wait to see what you came up with. -**TB***

Notes

Business Tools

Now that you are armed with your company colors, theme, references and images it is time to equip yourself with basic tools you will need for your product or service.

1. **Website** *(skip if not applicable)*: If you haven't already done this when you picked your name on page.90 do this now buy your domain name.
    a. **Ipage** https://www.ipage.com: I use this because I have multiple domains and only pay one hosting fee for them all.
    b. **Bluehost** https://www.bluehost.com/: Another really good one that I know tons of my clients use. Great choice if you want to start a blog on wordpress.com.
    c. **Wix** https://www.wix.com: I love Wix and have some websites built on this platform. It's super easy to use.
    d. **Squarespace** https://www.squarespace.com: is another amazing platform for creatives to build their website. It is similar to Wix, so it boils down to preference.
    e. **Shopify** https://www.shopify.com/: Get for if the product you will be selling is clothes.
2. **Business PayPal Account** https://www.paypal.com/uk/webapps/mpp/merchant: This is a great all around way to keep track of money coming in and great for processing credit card payments.
    a. **Stripe** https://stripe.com/: a get add-on to having a PayPal account. You receive your

payment quickly and integrates while with websites and social media sites.

3. **Accounting:**
   a. **Freshbooks** https://www.freshbooks.com: Good for tracking time for consultants who need to bill clients.
   b. **Waveapps** https://www.waveapps.com/: Free and easy accounting, invoicing, and more.

4. **Design**
   a. **VistaPrint** http://www.vistaprint.com/: Great for Business Cards and more.
   b. **Fiverr** https://www.fiverr.com/: Great for logo's, book cover design, stationery design and so much more. (***Quick Note:*** *always check reviews before choosing someone to work with and always email them questions before you pay for a gig*)
   c. **Canva** https://www.canva.com/: Good for creating your layouts and other creative projects.
   d. **Pixlr** https://pixlr.com/desktop: Very similar to Photoshop.
   e. **Adobe Photoshop**: for professional photo editing. (you only need this if you know how to use it.)
   f. **Photo Grid** https://photogrid.org/: Great for making collages and can be used on all devices to include online.
   g. **Creative Market** https://creativemarket.com – Is a great site for themes, graphics, fonts and more.

5. **Free Conference Call** https://www.freeconferencecall.com/: This is great for all type of business needs, but the best part to me is that you can setup to record your calls and go back and

replay them if you missed something.

6. **Google (Voice, Email, Drive, Hangout, Drive, AdWords, AdSense, Analytics, Docs and more):** I am so Google everything, but the most important things you need to setup right away for free is Voice, Email, and Drive.

7. **Mail Chimp** http://mailchimp.com/ is a great email marketing tool that allows you to build relationships with your readers and keep in touch with them.

8. **Lead Pages** http://www.leadpages.net/: this is great for both product or services. It will help you grow your business by making it super simple to grow your email list.

<u>Notes</u>

Service Tools

When it comes to services, you don't need much, outside of a good website and amazing marketing to get clients. But you will need some key tools to keep your company on track and thriving.

1. **Skype** http://www.skype.com/en/ **(Free):** an online program that allows you to call other Skype users for free, anywhere in the world. Good for video calls with clients and used with many services like consultations, fitness training, one on one lessons, etc. You can get creative on how you incorporate Skype with your services.

2. **Call Recorder (ecamm)** http://www.ecamm.com/ **Mac Only ($29 one time fee):** Records Skype video calls. Use as a bonus for clients, by sending them a copy of their sessions with you.
   Pamela for Skype http://www.pamela.biz/ **PC ($17 - $45 one time fee)**

3. **Satori App** http://satoriapp.com/ **($29 - $79 monthly):** This is an amazing app coaching services. They provide you with a system that will do all the booking, scheduling, billing and more.

4. **Typeform** https://www.typeform.com/ **(Free – $70 monthly):** build amazing surveys that will help you understand your clients before and after you even meet them.

5. **Davinci Virtual** https://www.davincivirtual.com/**:** with 1000 locations worldwide this is a great solution for meeting clients in person without having the office overhead.

<u>Notes</u>

Product Tools

Whether you're selling a digital or tangible product the list below will be your guide to do this seamlessly.

Building A Store:
The following list below is great sources for selling products either sold directly by you or created by you, then uploaded and sold for you hassle free.

1. **Etsy** https://www.etsy.com/
2. **Storenvy** http://www.storenvy.com/
3. **Red Bubble** http://www.redbubble.com/
4. **Zazzle** http://www.zazzle.com/
5. **Society 6** https://society6.com/
6. **LightBox** http://amzn.com/B00DOGIKXG: Great for product shoots of small to medium products.

EBooks and Printed Books:
This list will not only help you in the process of creating your book. It will help you with distribution.

1. **iPages (Mac Only)** http://www.apple.com/mac/pages/: good for creating worksheets and eBooks.
2. **Word Doc:** good for eBooks
3. **Scrivener Software** http://amzn.com/B0079KJB54: used for writing and editing. Also great for organizing notes.
4. **Grammarly** https://www.grammarly.com/: good for correcting up to 10 times more mistakes than your

word processor.

5. **DPD (Digital Product Delivery)**
https://getdpd.com/: Allows you to accept payments and auto deliver digital products for you. And amazing features like affiliates programs, multiple price points, bundles, and integrations. Great for selling ebooks and worksheets.

6. **iBook's Author**
http://www.apple.com/itunes/working-itunes/sell-content/books/: Sell books on iTunes.

7. **Kindle Direct Publishing**
https://kdp.amazon.com/: Get your book on Kindle.

8. **Create Space** https://www.createspace.com/: this is the company you have to go to if you want to print on demand with Amazon.

9. **Ingram Spark** http://www.ingramspark.com/: Great company for all around self-publishing.

10. **Copyright** http://copyright.gov/

11. **Bowker (ISBN)** https://www.myidentifiers.com/: This is where you get your barcodes and book serial numbers so company's and even libraries can order your book.

Webinars and E-Courses:

If you are going to do webinars and e-courses, this should help you along the way and cut done a lot of time trying to figure out how to do it.

1. **Course Craft** https://coursecraft.net/: for hosting courses

2. **Skill Share** https://www.skillshare.com/: for hosting courses

3. **Google Hangouts on Air:** Good for webinars
4. **QuickTime:** Great for recording audio, video, and screencasts.
5. **iMovie (Mac):** Video Editing
6. **Windows Movie Maker (PC):** Video Editing
7. **Wistia** http://wistia.com/: is good for storing and sharing videos.

<u>Notes</u>

A lot of information I know! So to help you keep track of all your new accounts I have supplied you with a web address key. Feel free to make copies and use it over and over again.

Web Address Key

Web Address: _____
User Name: _____
Password: _____
Security Question: _____
_____

Special Info: _____
_____

Web Address: _____
User Name: _____
Password: _____
Security Question: _____
_____

Special Info: _____
_____

Web Address: _____
User Name: _____
Password: _____
Security Question: _____
_____

Special Info: _____
_____

Web Address: _____
User Name: _____
Password: _____
Security Question: _____
_____

Special Info: _____
_____

Web Address Key

Web Address: _____
User Name: _____
Password: _____
Security Question: _____
_____
Special Info: _____
_____

Web Address: _____
User Name: _____
Password: _____
Security Question: _____
_____
Special Info: _____
_____

Web Address: _____
User Name: _____
Password: _____
Security Question: _____
_____
Special Info: _____
_____

Web Address: _____
User Name: _____
Password: _____
Security Question: _____
_____
Special Info: _____
_____

Step 5 at a Glance

You now have everything you need to get down to the core of your work. In Step 5 you do the work to create and setup everything you need to start selling.

Answer or just keep in mind the questions asked below.

1. Where do you want to start in the process? (ex. Order products, build website, write book intro, do photoshoot)

2. What will your artwork look like for your product?

3. Will you need help from outside resources?

<u>Notes</u>

"*Start where you are.
Use what you have.
Do what you can.*"
-Arthur Ashe

82

The Take Off

Step 5

Welcome to the easy part, I promise. You've already done the work, and you know everything you are going to need. So now it's time to "Just Do It!" as Nike would say.

In step 5 you will break up the work into four parts. You don't have to do it in any order; you just have to complete it. For this part, I want you to turn off all distractions and come up with a strategy. If you are selling a product, you need to order; Setup a time and date to pick and place the order. If you are going to sell a service, you should start working on what you will be offering and a great video as your sales pitch.

Tips

1. Turn off all distractions
2. Go back in the workbook to **pages 28-30**, and **50**. Use these pages as a reference.
3. Also, use all the information you collected in your Theme, Images, and References folders
4. You don't have to do anything in order, just write a list of everything that needs to be done, then break it up in fours.
5. When you are writing do not stop to fix any grammar, just write. I want you to keep the creative juices following.
6. If you have calls to make to order or set things up. Do it first thing in the morning when there are fewer distractions.
7. If you run into things that require more research and "fact checking" write it down in the notes sections but don't stop until you have done all the work.
8. If you are saying "I am not a writer, but I know everything I want to say." Well, you can get a small recorder and just talk. Say everything you want to express on it and then you can have it sent out to a transcriber.
9. If you need to tape videos and are not sure how and where to start, go on YouTube. You can learn how to record on your phone and edit with free software until your brand grows and start making revenue.
10. Avoid using jargon in your work so that your potential clients don't feel dumb.
11. If you are doing, instructional videos use the notes section to script what you are going to say before you start.

To Do

Now take the time and write everything you will need to do
to get your product/service to market.

1.

2.

3.

4.

5.

6.

7.

8.

9.

10.

11.

12.

13.

14.

15.

16.

17.

18.

19.

20.

Now break it up into four parts:

1st 1 of 4

1.

2.

3.

4.

5.

2nd 2 of 4

6.

7.

8.

9.

10.

3rd 3 of 4

11.

12.

13.

14.

15.

4th 4 of 4

16.

17.

18.

19.

20.

1st 1 of 4

<u>Notes</u>

"*Don't compare your* CHAPTER 1 to *someone else's* CHAPTER 20."

- *unknown*

2nd 2 of 4

<u>Notes</u>

"*There is no one giant step that does it; it's a lot of little steps.*"

-*Peter A. Cohen*

3rd 3 of 4

Notes

"*Like a piece in a puzzle, you have a unique position to occupy.*"

-Spirit View

4th 4 of 4

<u>Notes</u>

Finishing Touches

You have done so much work, and I am so proud of you! Now it's time to go through your work and do the following:

1. Rewrite any unclear words

2. Edit your writing

3. Edit your videos

4. Edit website layout

5. Research any facts or references needed for your work

6. Ask three friends or family members to review your work and make changes accordingly.

7. Hire a professional editor to make final edits (only if needed).

8. Ask yourself does it look and feel the way you want it?

9. How can you make it better?

10. Does it naturally answer questions people will have?

Congratulations
You did it!

Quick Break: *Jump on social media and share your news with the world that you **#StopTheBS** and did it! You completed the process of creating something great and are prepping to share it with the world soon. Don't forget to tag me too **@TracyBalan** – Can't wait to see what you came up with. -TB*

Step 6 at a Glance

You now have finished creating your product/service, but there are still some things that need to be finished before you can make "**BANK**". You need to price out what your time, product/service is worth. In Step 6 I will teach you how to price your product/service at the right prices.

Answer or just keep in mind the questions asked below.

1. How much will it cost you to run your total business monthly? Year?

2. What are your competitor's prices? (You should have the answer for this on **page.25**)

3. Will your prices reflect the quality of your product/service? (Meaning: Are you going set your prices based on work or to beat the competition?)

Notes

"Money won't create
success, the freedom
to make it will."

-Nelson Mandela

Pricing Guide

Step 6

Okay so the work is done, Yayyyyyyyy! Now, how much do you want to get paid for said work? It's time to find out what's your worth.

Your pricing will send a message to potential clients; it will imply the value or your services/products. The end goal when setting your prices will be not to cheat yourself while making the client feel they have won too.

So get out your calculators and pencils and let's come up with the perfect formula on how to figure this out.

Similar Products

When you are looking at your competitor's prices, make sure you don't find the lowest priced things. And make yours cost less. Instead, I like to price my items on the medium to high end. If I see that they are selling something similar for $50 - $100, I am going to price mine at $75 - $125. You may be asking: "Why more?" because I know I have a better quality product/service.

You must remember this when comparing your product/service to your competitor's: "Buyers Perception."

If you are saying to potential clients that you have the better product/service, then why is it cheaper? Yes, most buyers do not want to be overcharged for anything. But most buyers will pay more if they perceive that they are getting more at that higher price. Do you understand?

Here's another example:

Why are Louboutin shoes more expensive than Payless shoes? Because Louboutin, sold you on the idea that they only make the most superior quality shoes. Where Payless is selling you the idea of getting the look for less. The Same type of items but two different demographics.

"Quality is remembered long after the price is forgotten."
– Gucci

Price Calculator

First, let's define some word, so I don't lose you as we go through the price calculator to come up with the best prices.

Vocabulary

Labor: The hours you expect to work for the year.

Overhead Expenses: This includes, shipping supplies, onetime expenses and even travel expenses.

Materials Cost: Either the cost of the item from the supplier or the total cost of the raw materials used to make your product or setup your service.

Profit: The markup number after you have factored in your costs.

Wholesale: Items sold to others because they are buying in high volumes and are entitled to better prices so that they can resell at a marked up price.

How to calculate:

Labor + Expenses + Materials x 2 = Wholesale

Labor + Expenses + Materials x 4 = Retail

Examples:

Labor:
Let's say I only want to work 20hrs a week for the next 12 months and want to pay myself an hourly rate of $25 hr.

20 hours' weekly x $25 hourly = $500 Weekly
$500 weekly x 4 weeks = $2000 Monthly
$2000 monthly x 12 months = $24,000 Yearly

Overhead Expenses:
Let's say I spend $6,000 a year running my business.

$6,000 Yearly
$6,000 yearly / 12 months = $500 monthly
$500 monthly / 4 weeks = $125 weekly
$125 Weekly / 20 hrs. = $6.25 hourly

Material Cost:
Let's say I am selling necklaces and get them at a price of $3 each. I expect to sell 150 pieces a month and 1800 pieces a year.

150 pieces' x $3 per necklace = $450 monthly
$450 monthly x 12 months = $5,400 yearly

Profit:

When wholesaling, you should always sell at two times the price.

When retail selling you should always be at four times the price.

Now let's work out your final numbers

Note that for each piece I sell it only takes me 15 mins to package and ship out which factors my labor cost per piece to:

$25 hourly / 4 (15 min increments) = $6.50 for 15mins

Also, note that my expenses should be factored by that 15 mins too:

$6.25 hourly / 4 (15 min increments) = $1.57 for 15mins

Labor + Expenses + Materials x 2 = Wholesale

Wholesale Price
$6.50 + $1.57 + $3 = $11.07 x 2 = $22.14

Labor + Expenses + Materials x 4 = Retail

Retail Price
$6.50 + $1.57 + $3 = $11.07 x 4 = $44.28

So as you see I 've covered all my expenses and paid myself. I have even earned enough to reinvest into my company with left over to save.

Notes

Things to Remember

The list below are things that you should always remember when you are doing your calculations.

Labor:
- Hours spent creating
- Hours spent buying/ordering product
- Hours spent with client consulting
- Hours spent with client
- Hours spent doing follow-ups
- Hours spent adverting, marketing and social media

Expenses:
- Laptop
- Books
- Printer and Ink
- Mailing Fees
- Cell Phone
- PayPal / Strip fees
- Office Supplies
- Website domain and hosting fees
- Promotional material and Ad campaigns
- Travel fees

Materials:
- Original cost of products
- Business cards
- Packaging supplies

"The cost of being wrong is less than the cost of doing nothing."

– Seth Godin

Step 7 at a Glance

Can you believe it you are down to one last step? Step 7 is all about market and promotion. You will learn great tips to get your product/service out there. I know you didn't spend all this time creating for yourself, not to make a profit, Right?

Answer or just keep in mind the questions asked below.

1. Who will be your early supporters?

2. Will your new product/service create excitement?

3. What social media platforms, are you going use to promote your product/service?

4. What kind of giveaways will you give out to your new buyers?

5. Will you offer any incentive plans? Ex. Affiliates programs or discounts or deals for referrals?

6. Will you spend money on advertisement?

Notes

"*Ninety percent of selling is conviction, and 10 percent is persuasion.*"

-*Shiv Khera*

Sales
&
Promotion

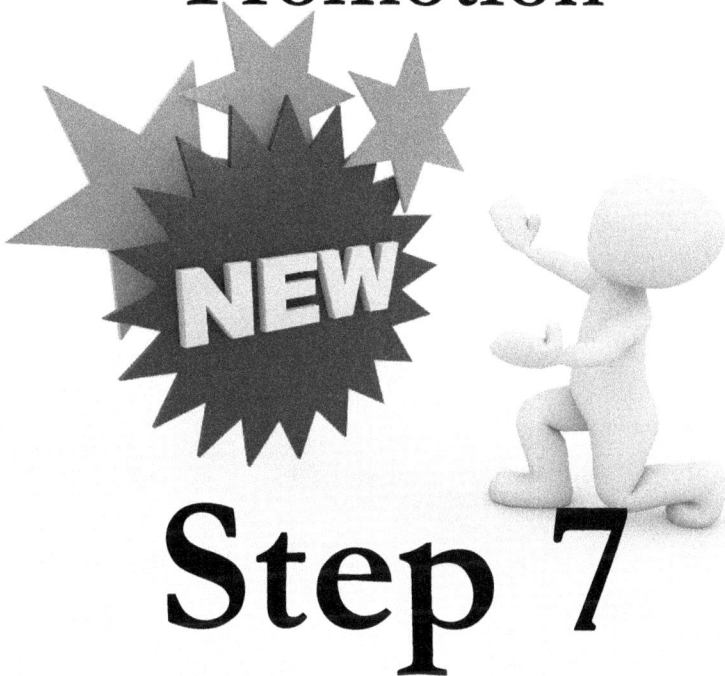

Step 7

Welcome to the finish line! Where you learn about the sales and promotion of your products/services to make **"BANK."**. It will be fun coming up with giveaways and cool ways to display your products /services to the masses. This step is all about creating excitement.

Let's get started because I don't know how much longer your future clients can wait!

Sales Copy

Definition: *A sales copy is the text you use to persuade your readers to take a specific action.*

The ability to write a great sales copy is the most important marketing skill you can learn. Even for visual channels like YouTube you still need to write a compelling headline to get people to view your video.

A good sales copy is:

Engaging: it focuses on reader benefits;
Clear: it is easy to read and easy to understand;
Concise: sales copy doesn't use more words than necessary;
Persuasive: it encourages a reader to take action.

You know your sales copy is good if your readers take the action you want them to take!

Remember always to answer this question:

"Why should I care?"

Because

_____

_____

_____

_____

Soft Launch

Definition: A soft launch is the release of a new product or service to a restricted audience or market in advance of a hard launch.

Now that you understand what a soft launch is, you are probably wondering "Why is it good to do one?"

A soft launch gives you time to work out all the kinks. You will only release your new product/service to the supports you already have (friends, family, fans, past, clients, coworkers, mentors, etc.) at a discounted rate for their honest feedback and to provide testimonials. You then should take that feedback and fine tune your new product/service before your hard launch.

Soft Launch Checklist:

(I have lift spaces open below for you to add additional things to the list.)

☐ Sales copy
☐ Discount codes for soft launch buyers
☐ Logo
☐ Product/Service elevator pitch
☐ Clear understanding of your ideal customers
☐ "About You "written and add to website
☐ Professional photo for press releases
☐ The setup of all social media platforms you are going to use.
☐ Professional email account setup
☐ Email signature setup that includes a tagline and links to your products/services
☐ Email collection forms setup on website and social media accounts
☐ A "coming soon" promotional page setup with email signup form
☐ Two weeks of social media post schedule (I will be showing you how to do this in the pages to follow.)
☐ Affiliate program Setup
☐
☐
☐
☐
☐
☐

Affiliate Program

Creating affiliate programs can be super easy and are a great way to do both a soft and hard launch. Time and time again, it's been proven that creating an affiliate program for your products/services can be a great way to reach audiences outside of your own and increase product sales.

The best way to setup an affiliate program is to choose an e-commerce platform that already includes this option. I use DPD **(Digital Product Delivery)** https://getdpd.com/. It's easy to use, cheap and cuts out the hassle of having to calculate and pay each person one at a time.

When setting up affiliate rates, offer anything from 20 percent up to 50 percent commission. I say this because it requires zero percent work on your part and you will literally make money in your sleep!

During the soft launch and even when promoting after, it is a great idea to promote your affiliate program. Doing this once each month will not only attract new business but may even turn old clients into new sales representatives.

Launch Ideas

The launch of your new product/service is a very big deal, and I know all this work you have done already probably has you saying "Tracy, I have no more brain power to give you" so here are a few amazing ideas to help your launch be a hit. I will leave some space below just in case you reboot and have some ideas you want to add.

☐ Do a social media challenge that ends with a giveaway spreading awareness about your product/service

☐ Create a # hashtag to encourage customers to connect and share photos about your product/service. Also, a great way to collect testimonial and photos to share on your social media platforms.

☐ Give tips away that relate to your product/service. (when you give people good advice about something they start to see you as an expert and trust you when you say buy this.)

☐ Host a free webinar talking about your product/service. Do giveaways before, during and after to keep everyone engaged during the webinar.

☐ Send your product out or introduce your product/service to the tastemakers in the field that you are selling too. (A good review from a tastemaker can up your chances of increased sales when you launch.)

☐

☐

☐

☐

Hard Launch

Definition: *the general release of a new product or service to the public.*

You have done your soft launch and received some amazing feedback. It's time to take that and spend some time fine tuning and adding the elements we talked about in the "Affiliate Programs" and "Launch Ideas."

There is no turning back with a hard launch, and I know you are ready. So go ahead make those changes and let's start to sell your wonderful products/services!

Hard Launch Checklist:

(I have lift spaces open below for you to add additional things to the list.)

☐ Launch date and time
☐ Attainable goals set for launch
☐ Payment system setup and working
☐ Final edits are done on all materials
☐ Full functioning website
☐ Added testimonials from soft launch
☐ Added reviews from soft launch
☐ Launch promotional items ready
☐ Launch graphics
☐ Launch email setup
☐ Email list setup of old customers and sales leads
☐ Promotional schedule setup and scheduled
☐ Discount codes for hard launch
☐
☐
☐
☐
☐
☐
☐
☐
☐
☐
☐
☐

Promotions

I have a surprise for you! If you did everything, I told you to do during soft and hard launch, guess what? You have already done half of your promotions. The checklist below are some extras to take you to the next level.

Promotional Checklist:

☐ Setup a Facebook business page – this is great doing Facebook ads which if do right gives you amazing returns

☐ Sponsor an event or charity that your potential customer might be a part of.

☐ Take part in social media groups where your potential customer might be.

☐ YouTube https://www.youtube.com/ – videos are a great way to drive traffic back to your site. It does not have to be super long just 3- 5 minutes. Just make sure it's interesting and drives them back to your site.

☐ Guest post on other websites like blogs, online magazines, maybe even print.

☐ Use Local Measure https://www.getlocalmeasure.com/ - a web-based service that collect's public data from social media platforms to find out who your customers are and lets you connect with them.

☐ Use Hootsuite https://hootsuite.com/ - to manage your social media. This tool can do update statuses on a variety of social media networks simultaneously.

☐ Create your own press releases and share it on the

following sites:
- o http://www.pr.com/
- o https://www.prbuzz.com/
- o http://www.free-press-release.com/
- o http://www.newswiretoday.com/
- o https://www.newswire.com/

Below is an example of a social media calendar I love to use. I have also supplied you with a blank copy that you can use over and over again to schedule your post. Make sure to make copies!

	S	M	T	W	TH	F	S
Twitter	1-3pm	1-3pm		1-3pm		2-3pm	1-3pm
Facebook			7-8pm	7-8pm			
Blog		11am				11am	
Guest Blog	7pm						
Pinterest	8-11pm			1p-3pm			2-4pm
Instagram	12-1pm	12-1pm	12-1pm	12-1pm	12-1pm	12-1pm	12-1pm

S	M	T	W	TH	F	S

Notes

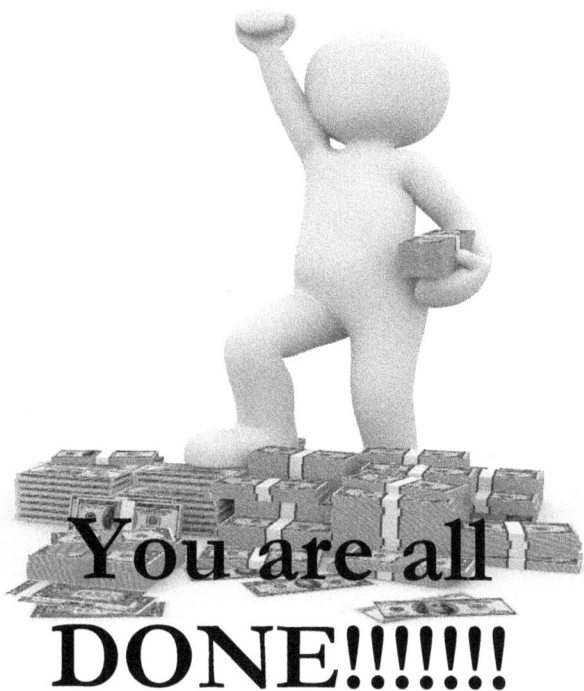

You are all
DONE!!!!!!!
And guess what?
One step closer to
"BANK"

Jump on social media and share your news with the world that you #StopTheBS and did it all! Let me know your release date and the links to buy so I can share it with my followers. Don't forget to tag me too @TracyBalan

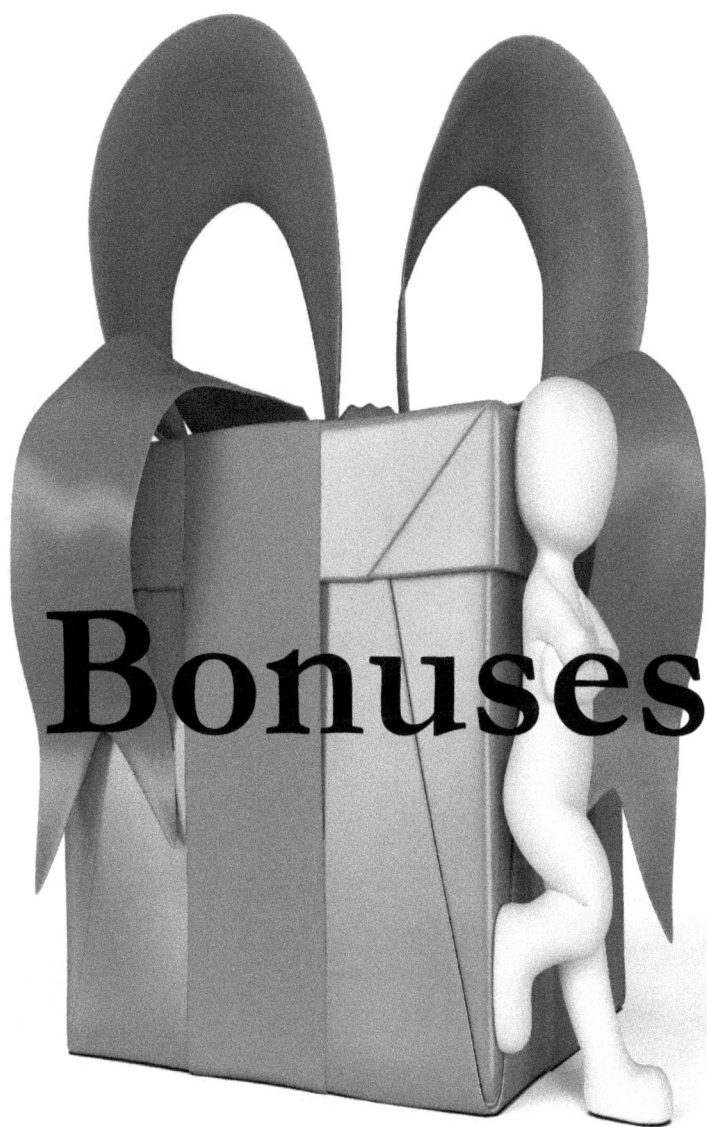

Bonuses

Did you think that after you did all that hard work, I would not reward you? Then you don't know your girl Tracy. I love giving gifts as much as I love getting them, lol! Enjoy the bonuses and let me know how you are using them.

☐ Time Management Log

☐ New Product / Service Production Log

☐ Video Storyboard Template

☐ Affiliate Networks

Time management log

Name: _____   Today's date: _____

Today's daily goals

Goal 1: _____   Goal 3: _____   Goal 5: _____

Goal 2: _____   Goal 4: _____   Goal 6: _____

Priority: A - Important; B - Somewhat Important; C - Not Important; * - Urgent

Time	Activity	Priority	Comments/results/energy

New Product

Requirements

Design

Build

Verify

Release

Video Storyboard

Title _____ Name _____

Video

Audio

Affiliate Networks

Don't just make money on your products/services, make money off the visitors on your website. Affiliate links are a quick and easy way to make money. By just adding a unique affiliate link to your website, you will generate a commission for every item purchased through your links. To help you get started, I have proved some affiliate networks below.

1. **Shopify -** https://www.shopify.com/affiliates

2. **Amazon Associates –**

   https://affiliate-program.amazon.com/

3. **Commission Junction** http://www.cj.com/

4. **Avant Link** http://avantlink.com/affiliates

5. **Rakuten Affiliate Network**

   http://marketing.rakuten.com/affiliate-marketing

Life is like riding a bicycle. To keep your balance, you must keep moving.

ABOUT THE AUTHOR

Tracy Balan is a Jack of all trades and the master of everyone! A gifted Brand Consultant, Beauty Expert, Motivational Speaker, Author and Television Host, with a resume that makes even the most talented professional quake in their shoes. Though her path to entrepreneurial excellence has been unconventional, every opportunity Tracy has embraced propelled her further up the career ladder to phenomenal success!

From business school to three years with the United States Military Intelligence Department to the prestigious Empire Beauty School. Then returning to get certifications in both Transitional and Life Coaching this Brooklyn, New York native never lost sight of her dreams to create a unique approach to consulting that has helped empower both companies and individuals to be more focused, balanced, and passionate about their brand and lives. Her signature brand of elegance, beauty, and straight talk has thrust her onto the world stage with a vengeance! No one who meets Tracy Balan will ever forget her.

Tracy is a seasoned consultant with more than fifteen years of collective experience in brand management and consulting, business management, leadership development, entrepreneurship, and marketing with a solid background in career and personal development to offer clients a unique, comprehensive and results-oriented approach to brand consulting.

As a brand consultant and motivational speaker, Tracy shares her story—the joys, the pain, the struggles and the incredible success and favor now lavished upon her. Her goal? To empower people around the world to pursue their dreams by teaching them how to be true to themselves. As the host of Lifetime's "Girlfriend Intervention", Ms. Balan has given notice to the world that she will not play small. She will play big, take center stage in their lives and teach them to go home with the prize! In her words:

"Find what works for you, not others. Then own IT!"

To learn more about the unstoppable Tracy Balan.
Visit: www.TracyBalan.com

www.ingramcontent.com/pod-product-compliance
Lightning Source LLC
Chambersburg PA
CBHW061322220326
41599CB00026B/4984